Calendar No. 457

114TH CONGRESS *2d Session*	SENATE	REPORT 114–250

CRITICAL INFRASTRUCTURE PROTECTION ACT OF 2015

R E P O R T

OF THE

COMMITTEE ON HOMELAND SECURITY AND GOVERNMENTAL AFFAIRS UNITED STATES SENATE

TO ACCOMPANY

S. 1846

TO AMEND THE HOMELAND SECURITY ACT OF 2002 TO SECURE
CRITICAL INFRASTRUCTURE AGAINST ELECTROMAGNETIC
THREATS, AND FOR OTHER PURPOSES

MAY 9, 2016.—Ordered to be printed

U.S. GOVERNMENT PUBLISHING OFFICE

59–010   WASHINGTON : 2016

Calendar No. 457

<table>
<tr><td>114TH CONGRESS
2d Session</td><td align="center">SENATE</td><td>REPORT
114–250</td></tr>
</table>

CRITICAL INFRASTRUCTURE PROTECTION ACT OF 2015

MAY 9, 2016.—Ordered to be printed

Mr. JOHNSON, from the Committee on Homeland Security and Governmental Affairs, submitted the following

REPORT

[To accompany S. 1846]

The Committee on Homeland Security and Governmental Affairs, to which was referred the bill (S. 1846) to amend the Homeland Security Act of 2002 to secure critical infrastructure against electromagnetic threats, and for other purposes, having considered the same, reports favorably thereon with an amendment and recommends that the bill, as amended, do pass.

CONTENTS

I. PURPOSE AND SUMMARY

The purpose of S. 1846, the Critical Infrastructure Protection Act of 2015 (CIPA), is to require the United States Department of Homeland Security (DHS, or the Department) to develop, regularly update, and submit to Congress a strategy to protect critical infrastructure against threats of geomagnetic disturbance (GMD) and electromagnetic pulse (EMP) and, to the extent practicable, to perform research and development and incident response planning to mitigate the consequences of threats of EMP and GMD.

II. Background and the Need for Legislation

Most of the nation's critical infrastructure depends on the electric grid to function, making the electric grid incredibly important to the nation's well-being, security, and economic progress. This massive distribution network is comprised of 390,000 miles of transmission lines, $1 trillion in assets, and 6,000 power plants.[1] The expansiveness of the grid also creates a broad attack surface and multiple opportunities for threats and hazards to disrupt the flow of electricity to end-users. Public utilities, economic production, and the health and well-being of Americans are impacted during significant disruptions to the electrical grid.[2]

GMDs generated by space weather and EMPs generated by the detonation of a nuclear weapon at high altitude are two separate threats that have the capability to severely disrupt the electric grid.[3] Either event has the potential to disrupt Americans' continued access to electricity. According to Lloyd's of London, a severe GMD could leave tens of millions of people without power for months or years and potentially cause economic losses topping $2 trillion.[4] Such an event is "almost inevitable in the future," according to the report.[5]

Defining the threats

"Space weather" generally describes "highly fluctuating magnetic fields and very energetic particles" in interplanetary space that cause "collective, often violent, changes in the space environment around Earth."[6] Also referred to as "solar storms,"[7] this activity is often generated by the Sun, which can eject plasma and magnetic particles that strike the Earth's atmosphere and can cause disturbances—known as geomagnetic disturbances, or GMDs—in the Earth's magnetic fields.[8] The magnitude, speed, and trajectory of the ejection all play an important role in how strong the resulting GMD may be.[9]

Separately, a high-altitude nuclear explosion can create an EMP consisting of an "intense steep-front, short-duration transient electromagnetic field, followed by a geomagnetic disturbance with tens of seconds of duration."[10] Like a radio wave, propagation of an EMP is dependent on its altitude and power—generally, an EMP detonated higher in the atmosphere will affect a wider area than

---

[1] U.S. Dep't of Energy, Large Power Transformers and the U.S. Electric Grid 5 (2014) [hereinafter Large Power Transformers], *available at* http://energy.gov/sites/prod/files/2014/04/f15/LPTStudyUpdate-040914.pdf.

[2] *See, e.g.,* Report of the Commission to Assess the Threat to the United States from Electromagnetic Pulse (EMP) Attack: Critical National Infrastructures (2008) [hereinafter EMP Commission Report], *available at* http://www.empcommission.org/docs/A2473-EMP_Commission-7MB.pdf.

[3] Lloyd's, Solar Storm Risk to the North American Electric Grid (2013) [hereinafter Solar Storm Risk], *available at* https://www.lloyds.com/news-and-insight/risk-insight/library/natural-environment/solar-storm; EMP Commission Report, *supra* note 2.

[4] *See id.*

[5] Lloyd's, Solar Storm Risk, *supra* note 3, at 4.

[6] Daniel N. Baker, Science, How to cope with space weather (Aug. 30, 2002), *available at* http://science.sciencemag.org/content/297/5586/1486.summary.

[7] Dan McMorrow, MITRE Corp., Impacts of Severe Space Weather on the Electric Grid 23 (2011) [hereinafter Impacts of Severe Space Weather].

[8] Space Weather Prediction Center, National Oceanic and Atmospheric Administration, Geomagnetic Storms, http://www.swpc.noaa.gov/phenomena/geomagnetic-storms.

[9] *Id.*

[10] P.R. Barnes, et al., Oak Ridge Nat'l Laboratory, Electromagnetic Pulse Research on Electric Power Systems: Program Summary and Recommendations xv (1993), *available at* http://web.ornl.gov/info/reports/1993/3445605662155.pdf [hereinafter Barnes EMP Report].

one detonated closer to the surface of the planet.[11] For example, an EMP resulting from the detonation of a nuclear weapon hundreds of miles above the United States could cover the entire contiguous United States.[12]

Potential impact on transformers

Like a GMD caused by a severe solar storm, a high-altitude nuclear explosion leading to an EMP could put the electric grid "out of service for periods measured in months to a year or more," according to the congressionally-chartered Commission to Assess the Threat to the United States from Electromagnetic Pulse (EMP) Attack, or "EMP Commission."[13] The same report states that widespread failure of large power transformers, or LPTs, could result.[14]

High-altitude EMPs and high intensity GMDs both create "geomagnetically induced currents" (GICs)[15] on the Earth's surface that can lead to major current and voltage fluctuations in anything on the ground that conducts electricity.[16] The effect is most notable in long conductors, especially long power lines and pipelines, since the induced current accumulates over the length of the conductor.[17]

Because LPTs are found at the end of long, high-voltage transmission lines, they are susceptible to damage from the cumulative effect of current and voltage changes resulting from GICs.[18] These transformers have a vital role in high-voltage transmission of electricity across the nation. They "step up," or increase, the voltage of electricity entering transmission lines, which is more efficient for long distance transmission, and "step down," or decrease, the voltage for distribution to end-users, who require lower voltages. Estimates indicate that there are at least 2,000 to 3,550 extra-high-voltage LPTs across the United States.[19]

Protecting LPTs from credible threats is important to maintaining the integrity and operation of the electric grid. Strong GICs can cause LPTs to melt and undergo other disruptions.[20] Losing even one LPT can be very consequential, because replacing it is a major undertaking: LPTs can take over one year to build; weigh hundreds of tons; cost $2 million to $7.5 million each; and require solving major transportation issues to get into the right locations.[21]

These transformers are largely unprotected from high-impact, low-frequency threats, including severe electromagnetic threats,

---

[11] JAMES GILBERT, ET AL., METATECH CORP., THE LATE-TIME (E3) HIGH-ALTITUDE ELECTROMAGNETIC PULSE (HEMP) AND ITS IMPACT ON THE U.S. POWER GRID 2–14 (2010) (prepared for Oak Ridge National Laboratory).

[12] *See* BARNES EMP REPORT, *supra* note 10, at xv.

[13] EMP COMMISSION REPORT, *supra* note 2, at *passim*.

[14] *Id.* at 43.

[15] JAMES GILBERT, ET AL., METATECH CORP., THE LATE-TIME (E3) HIGH-ALTITUDE ELECTROMAGNETIC PULSE (HEMP) AND ITS IMPACT ON THE U.S. POWER GRID 2–45 (2010) (prepared for Oak Ridge National Laboratory).

[16] *See* IMPACTS OF SEVERE SPACE WEATHER, *supra* note 7, at 13.

[17] *Id.* at 39.

[18] *Id.* at 42.

[19] *See* LARGE POWER TRANSFORMERS, *supra* note 1, at 21; IMPACTS OF SEVERE SPACE WEATHER, supra note 7, at 41.

[20] *See* GOV'T ACCOUNTABILITY OFFICE, GAO–15–692T, CRITICAL INFRASTRUCTURE PROTECTION: PRELIMINARY OBSERVATIONS ON DHS EFFORTS TO ADDRESS ELECTROMAGNETIC THREATS TO THE ELECTRIC GRID 6 (2015) [hereinafter CRITICAL INFRASTRUCTURE PROTECTION], *available at* http://gao.gov/assets/680/671554.pdf.

[21] LARGE POWER TRANSFORMERS, *supra* note 1, at 7.

though some mitigation measures may exist.[22] While there are several industry-driven efforts to maintain an inventory of spare transformers that can be utilized for recovery, such initiatives do not fully mitigate the impact of the threats to equipment. Challenges in delivering and installing LPTs, their cost, and the lack of spare transformers at all locations with active LPTs makes a spare transformer inventory less than ideal.[23] Protecting these transformers and other assets before a major solar or EMP event is likely to be a more cost-effective approach than only planning for replacement.[24]

Leaving the electrical grid and LPTs unprotected from high intensity GMD could threaten broad areas of the country. According to a study by a major insurer, a high intensity GMD event could have a total economic cost of $600 million to $1.6 trillion due to damages inflicted on transformers.[25] Between 20 million and 40 million people could lose power for up to two years.[26] Other predictions of the impact of high intensity GMD have been more severe.[27] According to Joseph McClelland, Director of the Office of Energy Infrastructure Security at the Federal Energy Regulatory Commission, who testified before the Committee on July 22, 2015, one Oak Ridge National Laboratory study concluded a 1-in-100-year GMD event could "damage or destroy 300 high-voltage electric grid transformers, interrupting service to 130 million people, with some outages lasting for a period of years."[28]

Historical experiences

Major space weather events have occurred several times in recorded history. The largest recorded space weather event on Earth happened in 1859, largely before the electric grid or its mitigation measures existed, and when the planet's most extensive technology network was still the telegraph system.[29] Known as the Carrington Event, the massive solar storm and the resulting GICs sparked telegraph wires, shocked operators, and knocked out telegraph operations throughout North America, Europe, and parts of Australia and Asia for two days.[30] In 1989, another major solar storm caused the Hydro-Quebec power grid to fail within two minutes.[31] More than six million people lost power for nine hours, costing $13.2 billion.[32] Dr. Richard L. Garwin testified before the Committee: "I emphasize that a once-per-century event might occur next week; it

---

[22] IMPACTS OF SEVERE SPACE WEATHER, *supra* note 7, at 2. *See also* NORTH AMERICAN ELECTRIC RELIABILITY CORP. (NERC), HIGH-IMPACT, LOW-FREQUENCY EVENT RISK TO THE NORTH AMERICAN BULK POWER SYSTEM (2010), *available at* http://www.nerc.com/pa/CI/Resources/Documents/HILF%20Report.pdf; Peter Behr, *Regulators Assess the Ultimate Blackout Threat*, N.Y. TIMES (July 2, 2010), *available at* http://www.nytimes.com/cwire/2010/07/02/02climatewire-regulators-assess-the-ultimate-blackout-thre–82657.html.

[23] Industry initiatives include the Spare Transformer Equipment Program (STEP) operated by the Edison Electric Institute, and Grid Assurance, an entity created by several utilities for recovery and resiliency.

[24] IMPACTS OF SEVERE SPACE WEATHER, *supra* note 7, at 66.

[25] SOLAR STORM RISK, *supra* note 3.

[26] *Id.*

[27] IMPACTS OF SEVERE SPACE WEATHER, *supra* note 7, at 51.

[28] *Protecting the Electric Grid against the Potential Threats of Solar Weather and EMP: Hearing Before the S. Comm. on Homeland Security & Governmental Affairs*, 114th Cong. 12 (2015) (statement of Mr. Joseph McClelland) [hereinafter *Protecting the Electric Grid*].

[29] SOLAR STORM RISK, *supra* note 3.

[30] *Id.*

[31] *Id.*

[32] *Id.*

has a probability of 10 percent of occurring within the next 10 years."[33]

The world's experience with high-altitude EMP has been limited to several nuclear tests, such as those carried out by the United States and the Soviet Union during the Cold War. In one such test, known as Starfish Prime, the United States detonated a nuclear weapon 250 miles above the Pacific Ocean.[34] Although 800 miles from the detonation, a series of streetlights failed in Oahu, Hawaii, as breakers tripped in the wake of power surges resulting from the blast's EMP.[35]

The Soviet Union carried out a similar test around the same time over Kazakhstan.[36] The test caused the failure of a 500-km-long communications line and its protective equipment.[37] It also disrupted a 600-mile-long underground power line buried three feet underground and caused a fire in a city power generation facility.[38]

More recently, experts have raised concerns, including at a Committee hearing in 2015, regarding North Korea and Iran, which have orbited satellites over the United States.[39] According to former Director of Central Intelligence, James Woolsey, who testified at the July 22, 2015, hearing before the Committee, such satellites may be test runs for similar orbiters that could carry nuclear weapons and cause high-altitude EMP over the United States in the future.[40] Using a satellite to carry out an attack using high-altitude EMP "is easier than launching a long-range missile at a target on the Earth," according to former Director Woolsey.[41] However, a spokesman for the Missile Defense Agency of the Department of Defense has stated that interceptors used for missile defense are able to defeat nuclear weapons detonated in space equally as well as weapons aimed at ground targets.[42]

Industry groups emphasize the differences between the potential threats to the electric grid posed by EMP and GMD. Bridgette Bourge, Senior Principal with the National Rural Electric Cooperative Association, testified before the Committee that while low-level geomagnetic disturbances are experienced fairly frequently, "a nuclear-induced EMP is considered an extremely low-likelihood, high-consequence event."[43] Additionally, according to Ms. Bourge's testimony before the Committee, given the relative frequency of low-level GMD events, the North American Electric Reliability Corporation has developed industry reliability standards to address the

---

[33] *Protecting the Electric Grid, supra* note 28, at 27 (statement of Dr. Richard L. Garwin).

[34] BARNES EMP REPORT, *supra* note 10, at 1.

[35] *Id.*

[36] Yousaf M. Butt, *The EMP Threat: Fact, Fiction, and Response (Part 1),* THE SPACE REVIEW (Jan. 25, 2010), *available at* http://www.thespacereview.com/article/1549/1.

[37] *Id.*; V.N. Greetsai, et al., *Response of long lines to nuclear high-altitude electromagnetic pulse (HEMP),* 40 IEEE TRANSACTIONS ON ELECTROMAGNETIC COMPATIBILITY 348 (1998).

[38] Butt, *supra* note 36.

[39] *Protecting the Electric Grid, supra* note 28, at 72–73 (statement of James Woolsey, former Director, Central Intelligence).

[40] *Id.; see also* R. James Woolsey & Peter Vincent Pry, *How North Korea Could Cripple the U.S.,* WALL ST. J., May 21, 2013.

[41] *Protecting the Electric Grid, supra* note 28, at 73 (statement of James Woolsey, former Director, Central Intelligence).

[42] William J. Broad, *Among Gingrich's Passions, A Doomsday Vision,* N.Y. TIMES (Dec. 11, 2011), *available at* http://www.nytimes.com/2011/12/12/us/politics/gingrichs-electromagnetic-pulse-warning-has-skeptics.html.

[43] *Protecting the Electric Grid, supra* note 28, at 4 (written statement of Ms. Bridgette Bourge).

threat of geomagnetic disturbances to the electric grid, effective last year.[44]

Status of Federal action

Recognizing the vulnerability of the grid, the EMP Commission made 15 recommendations to DHS and the Department of Energy that would improve the grid's resiliency.[45] These recommendations include:

- Understand system and network-level vulnerabilities, including cascading effects;
- Evaluate and implement quick fixes;
- Develop national and regional restoration plans;
- Extend black start capability;
- Prioritize and protect critical nodes; and
- Assure protection of high-value generation and transmission assets.

DHS is the Federal agency responsible for leading the Federal Government's efforts to protect and secure our nation's critical infrastructure across 16 sectors from a variety of threats and hazards, including cyber and physical.[46]

According to GAO, DHS has undertaken several projects to address threats to the electric grid at large, but has not specifically addressed all of the Commission's recommendations.[47] The Government Accountability Office (GAO) has also found that there is uncertainty within DHS about which office should have ownership of Departmental efforts to study EMP threats. Additionally, the National Protection and Programs Directorate, the office tasked by the Department with managing and addressing the risks of space weather threats, has not identified specific roles or activities it performs to address such threats.[48] GAO states that neither DHS nor DOE has identified the most critical substations and transformers, a key responsibility under DHS's risk management framework.[49] According to GAO, DHS also has not fully taken advantage of opportunities to work with stakeholders in understanding the nature of these threats and discuss research priorities.[50] However, GAO also acknowledges that DHS "does not have a statutory obligation to specifically address [the EMP Commission's] recommendations."[51]

The Critical Infrastructure Protection Act requires DHS to prepare a strategy to protect the nation's critical infrastructure against EMP and GMD, informed by an intelligence-based review and comparison of the risk and consequence of all hazards facing critical infrastructures. The bill also requires the Department to incorporate these threats in national planning frameworks and to carry out an educational campaign on these threats to the extent

---

[44] *Id.* at 4.

[45] EMP COMMISSION REPORT, *supra* note 2, at 55.

[46] Presidential Policy Directive 21 (PPD–21) directs the Department to coordinate with "sector-specific agencies" to carry out activities to protect and secure critical infrastructure from all hazards. The Department of Energy is the sector-specific agency for the energy sector. *See* Presidential Policy Directive 21, *Critical Infrastructure Security and Resilience* (Feb. 12, 2013); Exec. Order No. 13,636, 78 Fed. Reg. 11,739 (Feb. 19, 2013).

[47] *Protecting the Electric Grid, supra* note 28, at 23–24 (statement of Christopher P. Currie, Director, Homeland Security and Justice, U.S. Government Accountability Office).

[48] CRITICAL INFRASTRUCTURE PROTECTION, *supra* note 20 at 10.

[49] *Id.* at 13.

[50] *Id.* at 14.

[51] *Id.* at 1.

practicable. Additionally, the bill requires the Science and Technology Directorate of DHS to conduct research on mitigating the consequences of EMP and GMD, to the extent practicable.

III. LEGISLATIVE HISTORY

On October 30, 2013, Representative Trent Franks introduced H.R. 3410, the Critical Infrastructure Protection Act. The act passed the House of Representatives by voice vote on December 1, 2014, but the Senate did not take up the Act during the 113th Congress.

In the 114th Congress, on February 25, 2015, Representative Franks introduced H.R. 1073, the Critical Infrastructure Protection Act. The act passed the House of Representatives by voice vote on November 16, 2015.

On July 22, 2015, the Committee held a hearing entitled *Protecting the Electric Grid from the Potential Threats of Solar Storms and Electromagnetic Pulse* to examine the nature and potential consequences of GMD and EMP to the nation's electric grid.

On July 23, 2015, Chairman Ron Johnson introduced S. 1846, the Critical Infrastructure Protection Act, with Senator Ted Cruz, and the bill was referred to the Committee on Homeland Security and Governmental Affairs. The Committee considered S. 1846 at a business meeting held on July 29, 2015.

At the business meeting, Senator Johnson offered one amendment in the nature of a substitute, which modified the original language to distinguish between GMD and EMP, and required DHS to incorporate intelligence-based analyses into its research and mitigation strategies. The Committee adopted the amendment and ordered the bill, as amended, reported favorably, both by voice vote. Senators present for both the vote on the amendment and the vote on the bill were: Johnson, Portman, Lankford, Ernst, Sasse, Carper, Baldwin, Heitkamp, and Peters.

Consistent with the Committee's order on technical and conforming changes at the meeting, the Committee reports the bill with a technical amendment by mutual agreement of the full Committee majority and minority staff.

IV. SECTION-BY-SECTION ANALYSIS OF THE BILL, AS REPORTED

Section 1. Short title

This section provides the bill's short title, the "Critical Infrastructure Protection Act of 2015" or "CIPA."

Section 2. EMP and GMD planning, research and development, and protection and preparedness

Subsection (a) of this section amends section 2 and 201 of the Homeland Security Act of 2002, adds a new section 319 and section 526 to the Homeland Security Act of 2002, and provides various implementation requirements for the new provisions.

The amendments to section 2 of the Homeland Security Act of 2002, as provided in subsection (a), add definitions of EMP and GMD.

The amendments to section 201 of the Homeland Security Act of 2002, as provided in subsection (a), require the Secretary to perform an intelligence-based review and comparison of the risk and consequence of threats and hazards, including GMD and EMP, to critical infrastructure and develop and submit to Congress a strategy to protect critical infrastructure from the potential threats of GMD and EMP. The strategy must be updated biennially.

The Committee intends this strategy to focus particularly on critical infrastructures within the energy sector, including the electric grid and critical assets needed to ensure the grid's operation. The bill provides the Secretary latitude to incorporate the strategy into existing recommendations, provided that any resulting documents clearly address the requirements in this section. The strategy should be informed, to the extent practicable, by the findings of the intelligence-based review of threat, risk and consequence facing critical infrastructures required by this section.

The new section 319 of the Homeland Security Act of 2002, as added by subsection (a) requires the Under Secretary for Science and Technology, to the extent practicable, to carry out research and development to evaluate risks to critical infrastructures from GMD and EMP, and identify opportunities for mitigation. The subsection prescribes the minimum scope of the research and development conducted under Section 319.

The section requires the Under Secretary to consult with relevant Federal and industry stakeholders on the research required by this section. The Under Secretary should build upon existing Federal and nonfederal research, such as that performed or commissioned by the national laboratories and industry associations, to understand the risk posed by EMP and GMD threats relative to all other threats and hazards facing the grid. Research and development required by this section should evaluate and analyze a range of alternative approaches in order to improve the resilience of the electric grid. Incorporating real-world operational and cost data into this analysis would likely prove to be a valuable asset to research regarding the analysis of technology options for resiliency.

The new section 526 of the Homeland Security Act of 2002, as added by subsection (a), requires the Secretary, to the extent practicable, to create an incident annex or other response strategy that would guide the response to a major GMD or EMP event. The Secretary would have the authority to incorporate the annex or response strategy for GMD and EMP into an existing document. The new section 526 also requires the Secretary, to the extent practicable, to conduct outreach to educate owners and operators of critical infrastructure, emergency planners, and emergency response providers at all levels of government about the threats of GMD and EMP.

The Committee intends the Secretary to incorporate into the response plan the results of the required research on the various restoration and recovery capabilities of critical infrastructure under several GMD and EMP scenarios.

Subsection (b) of the bill includes technical and conforming amendments to the Homeland Security Act of 2002.

Subsection (c) provides a one-year deadline for the Secretary to submit to Congress the strategy to protect and prepare critical infrastructure against the threats of EMP and GMD.

Subsection (d) directs the Secretary to report to Congress on the progress made in addressing requirements in the bill, such as the requirements to conduct research and development to mitigate the consequences of threats of EMP and GMD, and outreach to emergency planners and emergency response providers regarding the threats of EMP and GMD. The report must include estimated completion dates for requirements not completed as of the report date.

Section 3. No regulatory authority

Section 3 provides that the bill does not grant any regulatory authority.

Section 4. No new authorization of appropriations

Section 4 clarifies that the bill provides no new authorization of appropriations and that the activities required by the bill must be carried out to the extent practicable using funds appropriated under existing authorizations.

V. EVALUATION OF REGULATORY IMPACT

Pursuant to the requirements of paragraph 11(b) of rule XXVI of the Standing Rules of the Senate, the Committee has considered the regulatory impact of this bill and determined that the bill will have no regulatory impact within the meaning of the rules. The Committee agrees with the Congressional Budget Office's statement that the bill contains no intergovernmental or private-sector mandates as defined in the Unfunded Mandates Reform Act (UMRA) and would impose no costs on state, local, or tribal governments.

VI. CONGRESSIONAL BUDGET OFFICE COST ESTIMATE

AUGUST 11, 2015.

Hon. RON JOHNSON, *Chairman,*
Committee on Homeland Security and Governmental Affairs,
U.S. Senate, Washington, DC.

DEAR MR. CHAIRMAN: The Congressional Budget Office has prepared the enclosed cost estimate for S. 1846, the Critical Infrastructure Protection Act of 2015.

If you wish further details on this estimate, we will be pleased to provide them. The CBO staff contact is Mark Grabowicz.

    Sincerely,

KEITH HALL.

Enclosure.

S. 1846—Critical Infrastructure Protection Act of 2015

S. 1846 would require the Department of Homeland Security (DHS) to undertake research and planning activities to mitigate the potential consequences of electromagnetic pulses and geomagnetic disturbances—resulting from either intentional acts or natural causes—on critical infrastructure, such as public utilities and national security assets. DHS is currently carrying out programs similar to those required by the bill, and CBO estimates that implementing S. 1846 would not significantly affect spending by the department. Because enacting the legislation would not affect direct spending or revenues, pay-as-you-go procedures do not apply.

S. 1846 contains no intergovernmental or private-sector mandates as defined in the Unfunded Mandates Reform Act and would not affect the budgets of state, local, or tribal governments.

On July 13, 2015, CBO transmitted a cost estimate for H.R. 1073, the Critical Infrastructure Protection Act, as ordered reported by the House Committee on Homeland Security on June 25, 2015. The two bills are similar and CBO's estimates of the budgetary effects are the same.

The CBO staff contact for this estimate is Mark Grabowicz. The estimate was approved by Theresa Gullo, Assistant Director for Budget Analysis.

VII. CHANGES IN EXISTING LAW MADE BY THE BILL, AS REPORTED

In compliance with paragraph 12 of rule XXVI of the Standing Rules of the Senate, changes in existing law made by S. 1846 as reported are shown as follows (existing law proposed to be omitted is enclosed in brackets, new matter is printed in italic, and existing law in which no change is proposed is shown in roman):

UNITED STATES CODE

* * * * * * *

TITLE 14—COAST GUARD

* * * * * * *

PART II—COAST GUARD RESERVE AND AUXILIARY

* * * * * * *

CHAPTER 21—COAST GUARD RESERVE

Subchapter A—General

SEC. 701. ORGANIZATION

* * * * * * *

SEC. 712. ACTIVE DUTY FOR EMERGENCY AUGMENTATION OF REGULAR FORCES

(a) Notwithstanding another law, and for the emergency augmentation of the Regular Coast Guard forces during a, or to aid in prevention of an imminent, serious natural or manmade disaster, accident, catastrophe, act of terrorism (as defined in [section 2(16)] *section 2* of the Homeland Security Act of 2002 (6 U.S.C. 101 (16))), or transportation security incident as defined in section 70101 of title 46, the Secretary may, without the consent of the member affected, order to active duty of not more than 60 days in any 4-month period and not more than 120 days in any 2-year period an organized training unit of the Coast Guard Ready Reserve, a member thereof, or a member not assigned to a unit organized to serve as a unit.

* * * * * * *

HOMELAND SECURITY ACT OF 2002

SEC. 1. SHORT TITLE; TABLE OF CONTENTS.
   (a) * * *
   (b) TABLE OF CONTENTS.—The table of contents for this Act is as follows:

     *   *   *   *   *   *   *

     *   *   *   *   *   *   *

SEC. 2. DEFINITIONS.
   In this Act, the following definitions apply:
      (1) * * *

     *   *   *   *   *   *   *

      (7) EMP.—The term "EMP" means an electromagnetic pulse caused by a nuclear device or nonnuclear device, including such a pulse caused by an act of terrorism.
      [7] *(8) * * **
      [8] *(9) * * **
      (10) GMD.—The term "GMD" means a geomagnetic disturbance caused by solar storms or other naturally occurring phenomena.
      [9] *(11) * * **
      [10] *(12) * * **
      [11] *(13) * * **
      [12] *(14) * * **
      [13] *(15) * * **
      [14] *(16) * * **
      [15] *(17) * * **
      [16] *(18) * * **
      [17] *(19) * * **
      [18] *(20) * * **

     *   *   *   *   *   *   *

TITLE II—INFORMATION ANALYSIS AND INFRASTRUCTURE PROTECTION

Subtitle A—Information and Analysis and Infrastructure Protection; Access to Information

SEC. 201. INFORMATION AND ANALYSIS AND INFRASTRUCTURE PROTECTION.
   (a) * * *

     *   *   *   *   *   *   *

   (d) RESPONSIBILITIES OF SECRETARY RELATING TO INTELLIGENCE AND ANALYSIS AND INFRASTRUCTURE PROTECTION.—The responsibilities of the Secretary relating to intelligence and analysis and infrastructure protection shall be as follows:

*   *   *   *   *   *   *

*(1) * * **

(26)(A) To conduct an intelligence-based review and comparison of the risk and consequence of threats and hazards, including GMD and EMP, facing critical infrastructures, and prepare and submit to the Committee on Homeland Security and Governmental Affairs of the Senate and the Committee on Homeland Security of the House of Representatives—

    (i) a recommended strategy to protect and prepare the critical infrastructure of the American homeland against threats of EMP and GMD, including from acts of terrorism; and

    (ii) not less frequently than every 2 years, updates of the recommended strategy.

(B) The recommended strategy under subparagraph (A) shall—

    (i) be based on findings of the research and development conducted under section 319;

    (ii) be developed in consultation with the relevant Federal sector-specific agencies (as defined under Presidential Policy Directive–21) for critical infrastructures;

    (iii) be developed in consultation with the relevant sector coordinating councils for critical infrastructures;

    (iv) be informed, to the extent practicable, by the findings of the intelligence-based review and comparison of the risk and consequence of threats and hazards, including GMD and EMP, facing critical infrastructures conducted under subparagraph (A); and

    (v) be submitted in unclassified form, but may include a classified annex.

(C) The Secretary may, if appropriate, incorporate the recommended strategy into a broader recommendation developed by the Department to help protect and prepare critical infrastructure from terrorism, cyber attacks, and other threats and hazards if, as incorporated, the recommended strategy complies with subparagraph (B).

*   *   *   *   *   *   *

TITLE III—SCIENCE AND TECHNOLOGY IN SUPPORT OF HOMELAND SECURITY

*   *   *   *   *   *   *

SEC. 319. *GMD AND EMP MITIGATION RESEARCH AND DEVELOPMENT.*

(a) IN GENERAL.—In furtherance of domestic preparedness and response, the Secretary, acting through the Under Secretary for Science and Technology, and in consultation with other relevant executive agencies and relevant owners and operators of critical infrastructure, shall, to the extent practicable, conduct research and development to mitigate the consequences of threats of EMP and GMD.

(b) SCOPE.—The scope of the research and development under subsection (a) shall include the following:

(1) An objective scientific analysis—

(A) evaluating the risks to critical infrastructures from a range of threats of EMP and GMD; and

(B) which shall—

(i) be conducted in conjunction with the Office of Intelligence and Analysis; and

(ii) include a review and comparison of the range of threats and hazards facing critical infrastructure of the electric grid.

(2) Determination of the critical utilities and national security assets and infrastructures that are at risk from threats of EMP and GMD.

(3) An evaluation of emergency planning and response technologies that would address the findings and recommendations of experts, including those of the Commission to Assess the Threat to the United States from Electromagnetic Pulse Attack, which shall include a review of the feasibility of—

(A) rapidly isolating 1 or more portions of the electrical grid from the main electrical grid; and

(B) training utility and transmission operators to deactivate transmission lines within seconds of an event constituting a threat of EMP or GMD.

(4) An analysis of technology options that are available to improve the resiliency of critical infrastructure to threats of EMP and GMD, which shall include an analysis of neutral current blocking devices that may protect high-voltage transmission lines.

(5) The restoration and recovery capabilities of critical infrastructure under differing levels of damage and disruption from various threats of EMP and GMD, as informed by the objective scientific analysis conducted under paragraph (1).

(6) An analysis of the feasibility of a real-time alert system to inform electric grid operators and other stakeholders within milliseconds of a high-altitude nuclear explosion.

* * * * * * *

TITLE IV—NATIONAL EMERGENCY MANAGEMENT

* * * * * * *

SEC. 501. DEFINITIONS.

In this Act, the following definitions apply:

(1) * * *

* * * * * * *

(13) the term "tribal government" means the government of any entity described in ⟦section 2(11)(B)⟧ *section 2(13)(B)*; and

* * * * * * *

SEC. 526. NATIONAL PLANNING AND EDUCATION.

(a) IN GENERAL.—The Secretary shall, to the extent practicable—

(1) develop an incident annex or similar response and planning strategy that guides the response to a major GMD or EMP event; and

(2) conduct outreach to educate owners and operators of critical infrastructure, emergency planners, and emergency response providers at all levels of government regarding threats of EMP and GMD.

(b) EXISTING ANNEXES AND PLANS.—The incident annex or response and planning strategy developed under subsection (a)(1) may be incorporated into existing incident annexes or response plans.

* * * * * * *

○